ALL
ABOUT
MYTHS

AFRICAN
MYTHS AND
LEGENDS

Catherine Chambers

Raintree

Chicago, Illinois

www.capstonepub.com
Visit our website to find out more information about Heinemann-Raintree books.

To order:
☎ Phone 800-747-4992
🖳 Visit www.capstonepub.com to browse our catalog and order online.

© 2013 Heinemann Raintree
an imprint of Capstone Global Library, LLC
Chicago, Illinois

To contact Capstone Global Library please call 800-747-4992, or visit our website www.capstonepub.com

Edited by Nancy Dickmann, Adam Miller, and Claire Throp
Designed by Jo Hinton-Malivoire
Original illustrations © Capstone Global Library, Ltd., 2013
Illustrations by Xöul
Picture research by Hannah Taylor
Production by Victoria Fitzgerald
Originated by Capstone Global Library, Ltd.
Printed in the United States of America in North Mankato, Minnesota. 042013   007335RP

16 15 14 13
10 9 8 7 6 5 4 3

Library of Congress Cataloging-in-Publication Data
Chambers, Catherine, 1954-
  African myths and legends / Catherine Chambers.
    p. cm.—(All about myths)
  Includes bibliographical references and index.
  ISBN 978-1-4109-4971-4 (hb)—ISBN 978-1-4109-4976-9 (pb) 1. Mythology, African. 2. Legends—Africa. I. Title. II. Series: All about myths.

BL2462.5.C49 2013
398.2096—dc23   2012017690

Acknowledgments
We would like to thank the following for permission to reproduce photographs: Alamy Images pp. 11 (© Interfoto), 19 (© Skakanka); Corbis pp. 4 (George Esiri/epa), 12 (Radius Images), 16 (Philippe Lissac/Godong), 18 (Nigel Pavitt/JAI), 39 (Robert Marien); Getty Images pp. 13 (© Achim Mittler, Frankfurt am Main), 17 (Gerard Fritz), 27 (Shem Compion), 29 (Jeffrey Oonk/Foto Natura/Minden Pictures), 35 (Berndt Weissenbacher), 41 (Sven Creutzmann/Mambo Photo); Rex Features pp. 5 (Victor Watts), 20 (Andre Csillag); Shutterstock pp. 24 (© Chris Kruger), 25 (© Trevor Kitteity); SuperStock pp. 28 (Eye Ubiquitous), 38 (De Agostini); The Art Archive pp. 32, 33 (John Meek), 34 (Dagli Orti); The Bridgeman Art Library pp. 6 (Lowe Art Museum), 21 (Look and Learn), 40 (James, Laura/ Private Collection); Werner Forman Archive pp. 7 (Musee Royal de l'Afrique Centrale Tervuren), 10 (Courtesy Christie's).

Background images: Shutterstock (©Galyna Andrushko), (©Pal Teravagimov), (©Igor Zh.), (©Joel Shawn), (©Nejron Photo), (©bonsai), (©Graeme Shannon), (©STILLFX), (©Konyayeva).

Cover photograph of a dancer in Tokolosh mask reproduced with permission of Corbis (Martin Harvey) and cover graphic Shutterstock (© Martin Capek).

The publisher would like to thank Mark Faulkner, Senior Teaching Fellow at the School of Oriental and African Studies, University of London, for his invaluable assistance in the production of this book.

CONTENTS

Did you know?

Discover some interesting facts about African myths.

Who's who?

Find out more about some of the main characters in African myths.

MYTH LINKS

Learn about similar characters or stories from other cultures.

AFRICA, LAND OF CONTRAST

Africa is a massive continent with huge contrasts in landscape, resources, and climates. The continent has a population of more than one billion, with many different peoples and at least 1,500 languages. Yet across Africa and beyond, myths and legends share certain themes. There are often powerful spirits, mischievous creatures, and heroic leaders.

MAKING SENSE OF IT ALL

Myths and legends are ancient tales that have helped make sense of Africa's gifts and challenges. They are often part of living faiths and traditions. Myths are the stories of spirits, creatures, ghosts, and other beings. They offer ideas about how the world began and why we behave as we do.

This festival on Africa's Atlantic coast celebrates Olokun, a great sea deity. Olokun is honored in the countries of Benin, Togo, and southwestern Nigeria.

Legends are ancient, fantastical tales usually based on real-life characters. They often tell of strong leaders who use supernatural powers to create great kingdoms. These stories give communities a firm sense of identity.

SHOWING A CULTURE

Some myths are magical and mystical; others are ghoulish and gruesome. Some legends speak of courage and daring, others of cruelty and oppression. Together, they show Africa as a continent bursting with cultural expression and a deep sense of history.

These are the ancient walls of Great Zimbabwe. More than 500 years ago, this was a thriving city. Many myths and legends surround its origins.

For how to pronounce African names, see pages 42–43.

MYTH LINKS

Trade and exploration have spread Africa's myths and legends across the world. For hundreds of years, the cruel slave trade took Africans far from their homes. In some of their new homes, such as the Americas, many African myths and legends thrive, though they have changed over time.

DEITIES AND SPIRITUAL BEINGS

People of many different cultures worship powerful spiritual beings such as gods and goddesses, or deities. In many African cultures, the idea of a spiritual being can also include nature spirits, ancestors, and others. No matter which name is used, these beings play an important role in African myths.

THEMES ACROSS AFRICA

Some ideas about spiritual beings are similar across much of Africa. For example, the cultures of East and Central Africa's Bantu speakers are very different from those of the Yoruba people of West Africa. Yet their deities hold much in common. Leza is a creator sky god honored by many Bantu speakers. Olorun is also a creator sky god, but from Yoruba traditions.

Figurines are carved to honor real and mythical twins. These are Ibeji carvings. An Ibeji is carved whenever a twin dies.

Did you know?

Twin deities often balance the forces of nature. For the Fon people of Benin, Liza is the strong, fierce god of the Sun. His twin, Mawu, is the cool, calm goddess of the Moon.

DEITIES WITH MANY FACES

Some deities have more than one identity. For example, Shango is the Yoruba god of fire. He is also the god of thunder, lightning, and sometimes war. Myths about Shango say that he was once a king on Earth. He killed people by blowing fire from his mouth.

Shango carries a double-headed axe or sometimes wears it buried in his head!

MYTH LINKS

Oshun is the peaceful river goddess of the Yoruba people. But in Brazil, Oshun has become a mythical goddess of love and beauty as well as waters. She is shown wearing jewelry and holding a fan. Oshun is honored by followers of religions such as Candomblé. These religions have African roots and developed among slaves taken to Brazil.

Trouble at the top: a Yoruba myth from West Africa

Eshu sat at the foot of the High God Olorun's cloud. He was feeling very restless.

"It's not much fun being a high god's helper. Olorun's always busy meeting other gods. There's nothing for me to do."

Eshu was so bored he leaned down over the heavens, staring at Earth below. There, he saw a teeming market with stalls selling vegetables.

Eshu felt jealous. People on Earth were always so busy *and* they had the fattest yams ever. Eshu suddenly felt hungry as well as bored. Then he had an idea.

Eshu grabbed a pair of Olorun's enormous shoes and tiptoed toward the high god's garden. It was full of the biggest, yummiest yams ever. Eshu dug up armfuls of them.

Back home, Eshu boiled up the yams and made them into smooth, delicious fufu. He left the fufu to cool while he secretly returned Olorun's shoes. He had just set them upon Olorun's cloud when he heard a great voice from above.

"Ah, Eshu!" cried Olorun. "I smell yams cooking! Aren't you going to share them with me?"

"Yams?" squeaked Eshu. "What yams?!"

"The yams that I, the great High God, know you took!"

"It wasn't me, oh High God!" pleaded Eshu. "Look! Look at the mud on your shoes! It must have been YOU."

Olorun stared at Eshu who was now looking scared.

"YOU accuse ME?" roared the High God. Then Olorun laughed.

"I need to keep you out of trouble, my friend. So I shall send you down to Earth every day. You'll return here at night and tell me everything that happens below. To help you, I shall give you all the languages of the world."

So Eshu traveled from heaven to Earth and back again—forever. He was never ever bored. And he enjoyed listening to gossip and creating chaos along the way. He is now Protector of Travelers, but would *you* trust him?!

HONORING THE GODS

Although most Africans also follow world faiths such as Christianity and Islam, festivals and celebrations for traditional deities and their myths are still held throughout Africa and in the Americas. The myths are acted out, sung, played, and danced. Images are painted, carved, and made into masks. Shrines are kept for mythical figures that still play a large part in people's lives.

Who's who?

Chibinda Ilunga is a hunter god of the Chokwe people, who live in Angola. His myth says he was descended from human kings. He married Lueji, a snake-king's granddaughter. They trekked far and wide, creating a great kingdom along the way. Chibinda Ilunga is often carved in solid wood. He has large feet to show his trekking skills and holds a walking staff in each hand.

ANIMAL SHAPES

Spiritual beings are often depicted in the form of feared and powerful creatures, such as snakes. Snakes shed their skins and emerge shiny and new. This is a symbol of eternal life. Danh-gbi is a life-giving serpent god from Benin. He is shown with his tail in his mouth, creating a circle, which represents unity.

Mami Wata is a powerful water goddess in west, central, and southern Africa, as well as the Americas. She is often shown as a mermaid with flowing black hair.

Did you know?

Masks and shrines can be made of wood, bark, cloth, raffia, gourds, beads, metals, stone, and plastics. White paint and pale cowrie shells represent the waters and foam of rivers and seas. The paint and shells decorate water deities and spirits.

THE SPIRIT WORLD

Many African cultures believe that alongside the human world, there is an invisible world where spirits, ancestors, and other beings are found. It's a bit like the idea of heaven and earth in some other cultures, but in African myth the human and spirit worlds are not so separate. The spirits can't be seen, but they can affect people's lives.

Did you know?

African sky gods can control both the good and the bad things in life. They are often held responsible for the weather. For example, a beautiful rainbow is often seen as a curse sent from the gods, because it signals the end of much-needed rains.

This rainbow will soon disappear. In some myths, the rainbow snake that created it will slink inside an anthill.

BETWEEN TWO WORLDS

In some stories, the human world and the spirit world are far apart, so deities might need help to communicate. Nyame, the Ashanti sky god in Ghana, gives much-needed rain to his wife, Asase Ya, who is Earth. The mischievous spider Anansi communicates between the two. In some stories, the two worlds are connected by a spider's thread or web, a great tree, or a tall tower.

Mount Kirinyaga, also called Mount Kenya, is home to the creator god of the Kikuyu in East Africa. Mountains are often seen as deities' homes.

Who's who?

About 40 Bantu-speaking groups honor Mulungu, a creator god who once lived happily on Earth. But violent people set Earth alight and killed many humans. Mulungu couldn't find the great tree to escape up to the heavens, so he scrambled up a spider's thread.

Wak's world: a myth from the Horn of Africa

Wak looked at the Moon and the twinkling stars in the heavenly home that he'd created. Then Wak looked down at Earth. He watched Man, the only being that he had made. Man was wandering alone on Earth's flat, dull surface. So Wak swooped down to make a few changes.

"Look, Man, I've had an idea," said Wak. "Take these planks of wood and make a box about the size of yourself."

Man looked a little doubtful but got on with the job.

"Now just get inside to check it for size," advised Wak. When Man was inside, Wak shut the lid and buried the box under the ground.

"Don't worry, Man!" yelled Wak. "Just have a quick nap while I give Earth a bit of a makeover."

Like many makeovers, Wak's took much longer than he expected. He spent seven whole years hurling rain and fire down on Earth to create mountains, valleys, and other beautiful features.

Afterward, Wak flew down to Earth and danced over the buried box until Man rose sleepily to view his new surroundings.

"Wow!" Man exclaimed, "Now all I need is someone to share it with."

"Aah! I've thought of that, too!" said Wak. "Come here! I just want to take a drop of your blood."

Wak used Man's blood to create a lively, intelligent woman. Together, Man and Woman created 30 beautiful children. But one day, Man saw Wak coming down to visit. He felt suddenly ashamed of so many children and tucked 15 of them into the folds of Earth.

Wak landed, looking puzzled and angry for the first time ever.

"So, Man, tell me where the rest of your children are!"

"Come on out, kids!" Man's voice wobbled.

Wak was furious that Man was ashamed of his own children. So he decided to punish him and all humankind. He remolded the children into animals and demons and...Death.

Wak returned to his heavens and Man never saw him again.

THE BAD AND THE UGLY

Creation isn't all positive. Creator beings and their helpers can punish humans or creatures for disobeying their wishes. They might send fire, thunderbolts, famine, foul diseases, and flood, to name just a few.

Creator gods and goddesses can perform miracles on Earth, although some are quite gruesome. Cagn is the creator god of southern African hunter-gatherers such as the Kung. His enemies brutally kill him, and ants strip the flesh from his bones. But Cagn is not a creator god for nothing. He puts his own bones back together again and covers them with new flesh.

Who's who?

Leza is a god of several Central African groups. In a Kaonde myth from Zambia, Leza orders Bird to carry three gourds down to Earth. But Bird must wait for Leza before cracking them open. Bird disobeys and splits them. Two contain seeds. But to punish Bird, the third contains ferocious beasts, disease—and Death.

■ Gourds are seed pods that are made into bowls and musical instruments. In myths, they can represent Earth or hide things, both good and bad.

The creator god for the Kenyan Luyia people made a gigantic red rooster. The rooster shakes his wings to send lightning, and crows to create thunder.

Did you know?

Some gods and goddesses produce living things from their stomachs. Bumba is the Central African Bashongo people's creator god. Bumba suffers severe stomach pains and vomits the Sun and water. Then up come the Moon and the stars, creatures such as leopards and tortoises, and finally humans.

HEROES AND HORRORS

Mythical heroes and heroines are not real people. But their myths are important to the communities that tell them. Tales often explain a community's traditional social groups and how they choose their leaders. Heroic myths can explain why one community always argues with another!

By the fireside at night, Hadza hunters from southern Africa tell myths of enormous kills that are simply unreal!

Did you know?

Myths often focus on features in nature that are important to people today. A mythical hero might cross a great river that now helps to irrigate crops. Tales celebrating mythical champions of hunting and bow-making honor similar skills that are still practiced today.

The Usambara Mountains in Tanzania were once great hunting grounds. Today, they are a popular tourist destination.

FROM ZERO TO HERO

Africa's heroic myths can be hundreds of years old and have many common themes. Often, the main character is cast out from their community. The hero returns as a leader through skill, daring, magic, and often, violence.

For example, the myth of Mbega tells how he was born into a leading clan of the Shambaa people in Tanzania's Usambara Mountains. Mbega is cast out of his home, but he uses his skills and magic to become a great pig-hunter and lion-slayer. Mbega wins many battles and becomes a great ruler for the Shambaa.

Who's who?

Mwindo is a famous mythical hero of the Central African Nyanga people. He was born from the palm of his mother's hand. The Nyanga king wanted to kill all his sons, but Mwindo survived. The hero and his sister, Nyamitondo, go on to rescue his people from the stomach of a giant bird that had gobbled them up!

Did you know?

Africa's heroic legends are usually passed down over generations by word of mouth. These are oral traditions. They are narrated, chanted, or sung as epic poems. The legend of Emperor Sundiata on page 22 is told by ancient families of griots from Mali. They perform with stringed instruments and xylophones called balafon.

Toumani Diabate is a member of an ancient family of griots from Mali. He is now an international star.

GREAT TALES OF REAL PEOPLE

Legends weave true deeds with mystical powers and unexplained happenings. Over time, narrators add fantastic details that make the legends more interesting for the people of their time. Most legends have some truth in history.

REAL HEROES WITH MAGICAL POWERS

Many of Africa's legendary heroes and heroines were real people, but stories often give them magical powers. These legends tell of battles, the creation of kingdoms, and how ruling families came about. For example, Shaka was a mighty warrior king of southern Africa's Zulu nation less than 200 years ago. His deeds have blossomed into legends.

This is Shaka Zulu (1787–1828). In legend, a blacksmith made Shaka a magical, powerful spear, which Shaka named Iklwa.

Who's who?

We know that 600 years ago there was a great warrior queen named Amina of Zaria, now in northern Nigeria. She led her army into battle and created a great kingdom. Legends say that as a baby she wielded a dagger like a soldier. As a warrior, she took a husband from every place she conquered, then killed him the next day!

Sundiata, the Lion King of Mali:
a Mandinka legend from West Africa

A young griot picked up his ballafon, tapped a tune on it, and started to sing: "Sundiata, the mighty Lion King! Sundiata, who changed from a weak child to a mighty warrior in just one day! Sundiata…"

"Oh, do be quiet!" snapped Sundiata. "You know perfectly well that I won't be mighty until our evil enemy, Sumanguru, is defeated!"

"Ah, yes," replied the griot and continued to sing. "Sumanguru the sorcerer-king of Sosso! He snatched Sundiata's half sister, Nana Triban! He grabbed the great griot, Balla! He…"

"Alright! You don't need to rub it in," interrupted Sundiata. "And don't forget that if Sumanguru hadn't kidnapped my faithful griot, Balla, you wouldn't have a job!"

Sundiata paced up and down with worry while the griot played a soothing tune on his ballafon. The peace was shattered by a great clattering of horses' hooves. Was Sumanguru attacking?

Sundiata dashed to the gates of the fortress, pushed his way past the guards, and looked up at the leading horseman.

"Balla!" he cried with joy. "My dear Nana Triban! How did you escape from Sumanguru?"

"I'll tell you later," she gasped. "We have no time to waste. I've found out how to crack Sumanguru's strength. You need to make a magic charm from a white rooster and attack him with it."

Sundiata quickly sent a messenger owl to Sumanguru, telling him to prepare for the battle of his life. Next, he chose a strong, sharp wooden arrow. He fixed the spur of a white rooster's claw to it. Then he and his soldiers thundered off toward Sumanguru's troops.

At the great battle of Kirina, Sundiata shot the arrow way up into the air. It swooped down, grazing Sumanguru's arm. With a howl of pain and terror, Sumanguru looked at the rooster's spur and felt all the strength drain from him. He knew he would be defeated.

Sundiata went on to build the great Mali Empire, which lasted for 400 years.

GIANT TALES

In many African tales, terrifying beings, including mythical giants, ogres, and mean spirits, create fear and confusion. In central Africa's deep Congo forests, there are fairies and goblins, too. Among the Zulu and Ambundu of southern Africa, ogres have wild, long, tangled hair. A few giants, though, are smiling and gentle!

The baobab is a giant of nature. There are many myths surrounding this "upside-down" tree whose branches look like roots.

MYTH LINKS

Giants appear in myths across the globe. Native American Shoshone traditions feature Dzoavits, who chases children—then eats them! Giants can be clever, too. In Jewish traditions, Og, King of Bashan, is the only giant to survive the Great Flood. He hitches a ride on the back of a unicorn towed by Noah's Ark.

THE OGRE AND THE DRUM

The East African coastal Swahili and the Southern Sesuto and Xosa share a myth in which an ogre hides a girl in a huge drum. She is rescued and the drum is filled instead with snakes, bees, and biting toads. The ogre cracks open the drum and the beasts kill him.

Drums are often played during the performance of a myth. Heavy drum beats can signal terror or the appearance of a scary character.

Did you know?

You can't see the wind, and you can't see a spirit either! In the Swahili language, the word *upepo* means both "spirits" and "wind." In West Africa's northern Nigeria, Hausa speakers use the word *iskoki*. The Hausa Maguzawa people once believed there were about 3,000 *iskoki* spirits.

CUNNING TRICKSTERS

There are many myths about tricksters, who use their cunning to outwit others. Some tricksters are deities or their helpers, like the Yoruba's Eshu. Others are human. But most tricksters are wily, funny, and sometimes shocking animal characters.

LINKING HEAVEN AND EARTH

Some trickster creatures run between the human and the spirit worlds, making mischief, like Eshu. Anansi is another such character. He is the son of Nyame, the sky god, and can appear as a spider or a man. Anansi uses his power to get the better of other creatures.

MYTH LINKS

African slaves took trickster tales across the Atlantic to the Americas. Here, they took on different names. *Anansi* is a popular character in tales from Ghana in West Africa. Anansi means "spider" in Ghana's Akan language. In the United States, Anansi changed to Aunt Nancy. In Haiti, it is Ti Malice.

TESTING AND TEACHING

Some cunning characters continually challenge the deities with their sly ways. Some of these tales are meant to show children that they shouldn't try to trick adults! Sometimes, though, the trickster wins. Those in power do not have the right to win all the time.

Did you know?

Did Anansi's wily ways come from Africa's real-life baboon spiders? There are about 40 species of this scary creature. Their hairy leg span can reach 6 inches (20 centimeters). They have a nasty, venomous bite, too. Some baboon spiders dig burrows and cover them with a silky web to trap their prey. Tricksy!

■ One baboon spider species hurtles down onto its prey and catches it in a web woven between its front legs.

HOW TO MAKE FRIENDS

Trickster tales warn us of the dangers in the world. Some of these tales are about friendship. Others tell us why animals look like they do. For example, one Swahili tale tells of Snake, who borrowed Millipede's eyes so that he could watch a wedding dance. In return, Snake lent his legs to Millipede. After the wedding, Snake refused to give back the eyes, and Millipede kept the legs. They are friends no more!

MYTH LINKS

Aesop's fables are trickster tales from ancient Greece, although some say that Aesop was of African descent. Many of these tales are about goodness. "The Lion and the Mouse" is about repaying kindness. "Don't rush things!" is the moral of "The Tortoise and the Hare."

Trickster tales are told or acted like a play. Each character has a unique voice. Props, drums, and other instruments add to the drama.

This is a small, quiet, and secretive water deer from the Congo Forest. In stories, the deer is called Nseshi and his character is quietly cunning.

Who's who?

Tortoise is a winner because he thinks slowly and carefully, but he isn't always nice. Hyena is greedy and often tries to take everything. In southern Africa, the jackal is smart and wins out in the end. But he's a scruffy, desperate creature.

HOW TO SURVIVE

Some trickster tales are also about African landscapes and seasons. They tell of times when life is tough, especially during the dry season. Food is scarce and tricksters survive only by their cunning or their wisdom. Many East African tales tell of Sungura, the Hare. He is often very hungry and has to use his wits to get food.

Hare, Hyena, and the pot of beans: a Swahili tale from East Africa

Hare and Hyena were friends. No one knew why. One day, when they had no work and were extremely hungry, Hare suggested they ask the Village Chief for a job in his garden.

The Chief was happy to hire them. "Here, take this pot of beans for your lunch!" he said.

As soon as they reached the garden, Hare made a fire and put the pot on to cook. At lunchtime, Hyena asked, "Could you just watch the pot, Hare, while I go down to the stream to wash?"

At the stream, Hyena stripped off his skin and hid it behind a rock. Then he dashed back to the garden.

"Aaaaaaagh!" screamed Hare when he saw this skinned ogre. And he fled into the grassland.

Hyena chuckled and gobbled up the beans. He then waddled back to the stream, put his skin on, and strolled back to the garden. There, he found Hare staring nervously at the empty pot.

"Where's my share of beans?!" thundered Hyena.

"A terrible ogre scared me away. He must have eaten them all up!" wailed Hare. "But I'm going to make a bow and arrow, and next time I'll kill the thieving beast!"

"I'm not sure I believe you, Hare," said Hyena. "Nevertheless, I'll help you trim your bow." But wily Hyena actually dug out a notch to weaken the bow.

The next day, Hyena played the same trick.

"I'm ready for you...you UGLY OGRE!" yelled Hare, pulling at the bow. SNAP! The bow broke and Hare ran off in a panic. Again, Hyena accused Hare of eating all the beans.

Hare protested wildly. Then he noticed that Hyena's eyes no longer had that hungry look in them.

"Hmmm," thought Hare. "I'll hide the next bow in the grass. I don't want Hyena's help."

The following day, Hare pulled the bow and...bull's-eye!

"Aaaaoooooow!" howled the wounded ogre, in a very Hyena-like way. He limped down to the stream then back to the garden. And there was happy Hare, eating ALL THE BEANS!

Brer Rabbit is wearing American clothes, but his character is similar to Sungura the African hare.

TALES ACROSS THE WAVES

We know that trickster tales were taken to the Americas by millions of African slaves. There, they adapted to life around them, and life was desperate. In Africa, Sungura is a smart but small and fragile hare. In America, he becomes Brer Rabbit, or "Brother Rabbit." Brer Rabbit is closer to being human than Sungura. He is also much tougher. These tales are about how to win, but the winner might behave very badly.

Did you know?

"Brer" characters came mainly from Carolina and Georgia in the United States. They were told in a language called Gullah. This is a mixture of West and Central African languages, and English. About 150 years ago, Brer tales were translated into English by Americans such as Charles Colcock Jones.

BORROWING FROM THE NEIGHBORS

Other characters in the Brer Rabbit tales are Brer Fox, Brer Lion, Brer Turtle, and lots more. These characters and their story lines are not only influenced by African stories. They have also taken in traditions from Native American trickster tales. This is a good example of how myths and legends absorb aspects of other cultures.

MYTH LINKS

The coyote is a trickster figure among the California, Plains, and Southwest Native Americans. Coyote also brings fire and other skills to humans and links the deities and Earth, like Eshu. Coyote can be very naughty but doesn't always win.

■ Brer Fox and Brer Rabbit are always trying to out-trick each other. Brer Rabbit always wins.

DEATH AND THE AFTERLIFE

All over the world, stories are created to explain how and why people die, and what happens after death. In Africa, there are many myths that tell of spiritual beings who brought Death. Others blame mischievous spirits or animals. Some myths involve all of them! Death can come from rulers of the underworld, too.

Lizard is a common character across Africa. He is often the bringer of death.

This is an African red toad. In myth, toads can pull people down to their death. In real life, toads are poisonous!

THE DEATH OF DEITIES

When deities die, humans know that no one is too great to escape death. Kibuka is a god of war and thunder among the Baganda of Uganda. The high god sends Kibuka to help the Baganda in battle. Kibuka is warned not to let his enemy know his battle positions, and not to talk to women. Sadly, he gets distracted by the battle. So he forgets the warnings, gets shot by an arrow in the sky, falls into a tree, and is the first god to die.

DOWN TO EARTH

The practice of burying the dead has led to myths that tell of porcupines, snakes, lizards, worms, burrowing animals, and other ugly beasts pulling people down to Death.

MYTH LINKS

Australian Aboriginal myths tell of the death creature, Yara-ma-yha-who. He has a large red head and sticks to fig trees with suckers on his feet. Yara-ma-yha-who waits for travelers to rest under the tree. He drinks their blood, then finishes them off. Later, he vomits them up again, only now they are a bit shorter.

The message of Death: a Lozi myth from Central Africa

High God Nyambe looked down at his dear, sick dog and watched him breathe his last. Nyambe was heartbroken.

"I know!" he cried. "I'll bring you back to life and you can live forever!" But then Nyambe made a big mistake. He turned to his goddess wife. "What do you think, Nasilele?"

"That manky old thing! No way. The dog stays dead," she replied.

Not long after, Nasilele's mother died. "Oh, Nyambe! Mother's dead! We must bring her back to life!" cried Nasilele.

Nyambe thought for about two seconds. "After careful consideration," he said, "I've decided that my dear mother-in-law should stay dead. We must set a good example to ordinary humans."

"But we haven't decided yet whether humans are to live or die," said Nasilele.

"You're right, we haven't!" replied Nyambe. "Let's sort it out."

So Nyambe and Nasilele talked through the night. Exhausted, they summoned Chameleon.

"In our great wisdom, we have decided that humans shall live forever. So you just run along and tell them," announced Nasilele.

Chameleon puffed up with pride. His skin turned a gorgeous glowing pink to match the dawn of the new day.

"All humans shall live forever!" he muttered as he leaped down onto the vast, dusty plain.

He ran past Lizard, who was hiding in the crook of a great tree. Lizard heard Chameleon repeating his message. Mischievous Lizard grinned and ran past Chameleon to the village where humans lived.

"Humans! I have a message for you from the heavens," Lizard called out.

The humans gathered in front of him and listened respectfully.

"The message is, 'ALL HUMANS MUST DIE!'"

From above, Nyambe and Nasilele looked on as Lizard gave a wicked laugh and shot back across the plain.

"Well, that's Fate for you!" shrugged Nyambe. "Come on Nasilele, we've got stuff to do. Now, what do you think about creating an animal with a hump that can carry things…?"

DEATH MYTHS LIVE ON

Today, African death myths are represented in masks, music, ceremony, architecture, and materials. For example, in Dogon myth, Lebe was the eighth son of the high god, Amma. One day, the seventh son swallowed him up and killed him. Then he vomited up the bones, which changed into stones as they fell. All the goodness of Dogon ancestors went into these stones, which represent Life.

Among West Africa's Igbo people, Ala is goddess of the underworld. When someone dies, they enter her womb. Ala is honored in houses called mbari. These are square with open sides and built by local men and women. Ala sends a bee, a snake, or another creature to show her priests where to build them.

The stone floors of traditional Dogon houses are seen as Lebe's bones. The roof represents the heavens. Together, Lebe and the gods of the heavens protect life in the home.

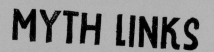

MYTH LINKS

Umbanda is an African-Brazilian religion. It is a mixture of Christianity, traditional African faiths and myths, and other beliefs. Umbanda's priests contact the spirits of dead people and Orixas, which are similar to West African deities. Omolu is Umbanda's Lord of Death and Disease. Priests ask him to save sick people from death.

Creatures can hold the spirits of the dead. The praying mantis is known as the "Spirit Bird." For the Khoi people, it is a trickster god that can be reborn many times.

MYTHS AND LEGENDS ALIVE

African myths and legends live on through traditional song, poetry, drama, dance, and ceremony. They have been transformed and are alive in the Americas today. Some have made it into modern culture through films and songs. Some legendary characters feature in computer games, like Shaka Zulu in "Civilization IV."

In 1994, Dani Kouyate made a film about Sundiata Keita, the king of Mali, called *Keita: the Heritage of the Griot.* In it, a boy experiences flashbacks to the times of his ancestor, Sundiata. Dani Kouyate's family are famous Malian griots.

In 2009, Daniel Schnyder composed music about Sundiata. Germany's Berlin Radio Symphony Orchestra and Malian griots performed it together.

The river goddess, Oshun, is celebrated every year. There is a ceremony for her at a sacred stream in Osogbo, Nigeria.

MYTHS AND LEGENDS OF TOMORROW

When does a special person, creature, or place become mythical? Will we see the stories of today woven with magic and mystery? When does a hero or heroine become a legend? Could it be a freedom-fighter and politician, like Nelson Mandela? Will it be a great musician or athlete? Can *you* think of anyone?

These Cubans are part of Santeria, a religious group combining Catholicism and West African religious beliefs. They carry a Christian statue that also has characteristics of the goddess Oshun.

Did you know?

In the 20th century, most of Africa was ruled by European nations. New myths gave Africans strength to fight for freedom. In 1905, Kinyikitile Ngwale led East Africans against their German rulers. He said that a strong snake spirit lay within him. His rebellion failed, but other Africans learned from it.

CHARACTERS, CREATURES, AND PLACES

Look at the words in brackets to find out how to say these African names.

KEY CHARACTERS

Amina, Queen of Zaria legendary soldier and empire maker. Zaria is now in northern Nigeria.

Cagn creator god of Kung hunter-gatherers from southern Africa

Chibinda Ilunga hunter god with big hands and feet, from Angola

Danh-gbi serpent god from Benin, West Africa

Eshu (Ey-shoo) mischievous messenger of the Yoruba high god, Olorun. He runs between heaven and earth.

Kibuka (Kee-booka) war god of the Baganda of Uganda. He was the first god to die.

Lebe (Ley-bey) god of the Dogon, Mali. He was swallowed and then spat out as stones.

Leza (Ley-zah) creator god of Kaonde in Central Africa. He sends a bird down to Earth with good things for humans but it all goes wrong.

Liza and Mawu twin deities from Benin

Mami Wata powerful water goddess from across Africa and in the Americas and Caribbean

Mbega (Mm-bey-gah) mythical hero, hunter, and fighter of the Shambaa people of East Africa

Mulungu (Moo-loon-goo) creator sky god of some East African Bantu-speakers, from the Kamba in northern Kenya to the Nyamwezi in Tanzania

Mwindo (Mwin-doh) mythical hero of the Nyanga of Central Africa. He is cast out from his country but wins out in the end.

Nasilele (Na-see-lay-lay) high goddess of the Luyi in Central Africa. With her husband, Nyambe, she accidentally brought Death to humans.

Nyambe (Nyam-bey) high god of the Luyi. With his wife, Nasilele, he accidentally brought Death to humans.

Oshun (Osh-oon) water goddess of the Yoruba in West Africa, and in the Americas

Shango Yoruba god of thunder, lightning, fire, and war

Sundiata Keita (Soon-dee-yata Kay-tah) legendary emperor of Mali, an ancient West African empire (different from today's country, Mali)

Wak creator god of the Oromo people from the Horn of Africa. He made humans, and then brought Death to them.

FEATURED CREATURES

Anansi (A-nan-see) spider trickster of the Ashanti in Ghana. He is often rather bad. He also features in tales from the Caribbean and the Americas.

Brer Rabbit African American tricksy creature, rather like Sungura of Africa. He is the main character in the Brer stories.

Brer Turtle, Brer Fox, Brer Wolf, and others all African American creature characters who try to outwit each other

chameleon across much of Africa, chameleon carries messages. Sometimes chameleon is good, while at other times, it is feared.

coyote mischievous trickster from Native American cultures

hyena wily creature from the Swahili in East Africa. He tries to trick other creatures to get what he wants.

nseshi (Nn-sesh-ee) tricksy water deer character from the Congo forest

rainbow snake across much of Africa, the rainbow snake can signal the end of the rains and the start of dangerous dry weather

Sungura (Soon-goo-rah) Swahili hare from East Africa. He is small but can outwit stronger creatures who try to trick him.

IMPORTANT PLACES

Great Zimbabwe ancient Central African trading city with myth and legend surrounding it

Mount Kirinyaga (Kee-rin-yah-gah) also known as Mount Kenya, in Kenya. It is the home of the Kikuyu high god, Mulungu.

Osogbo (Osh-og-boh) Nigerian city and home to Oshun, water goddess

Usambara Mountains home of the myth of Mbega, a mighty fighter and hunter

Zaria ancient trading city state, now a city in Nigeria. There are many legends surrounding it, especially about Queen Amina.

GLOSSARY

ancestors family members from long ago, who have died

Bantu group of languages with similar roots in much of sub-Saharan Africa. They extend from the border between Nigeria and Cameroon in the west, to the Swahili coast in the east.

clan group of people with family and cultural ties. Clans with the same culture together form part of a larger identity.

continent huge land mass

cowrie small shells used for decoration. They were once used as currency to trade for goods.

coyote wild, wolf-like dog from North America

deity god or goddess, usually referring to a particular people or culture

epic poem legend told in the form of a poem. It often starts out as spoken poetry before it gets written down.

fable story that is educational or has a moral meaning

famine long period of time with little or no food. People often die from lack of food during a famine.

fufu mashed root vegetables such as yams that are served with a sauce in West Africa

gourd hardened seed pod of the gourd plant or plants of the pumpkin family

griot West African musician and singer who tells ancient stories of great leaders

Horn of Africa area that is made up of the countries of Eritrea, Ethiopia, Somalia, Djibouti, and northern Kenya

hyena small, spotted, dog-like animal from Africa and Asia

irrigate supply water to the land to help crops grow

jackal wild, wolf-like dog from Africa

Khoi hunter-gatherer communities in southern Africa

ogre large, scary-looking creature that looks human

oral tradition histories passed down by word of mouth

praying mantis very large insect that holds its front legs in a praying position. It catches insects and bites off their heads.

shrine place built for people to remember spirits of deities and ancestors

slave trade trade in slaves from Africa to the Americas (including America, the Caribbean, and Brazil) and islands in the Indian Ocean, from the 16th to the 19th centuries. Africans worked on big farms called plantations in America. Slaves were treated cruelly.

trickster deity or character in myths who plays tricks and makes mischief

FIND OUT MORE

BOOKS

Fontes, Justine, and Ron Fontes. *Sunjata: Warrior King of Mali: A West African Legend*. (Graphic Myths & Legends). Minneapolis: Graphic Universe, 2009.

Green, Jen. *West African Myths* (Myths from Around the World). New York: Gareth Stevens Publishing, 2010.

Mckissack, Patricia. *Porch Lies: Tales of Slicksters, Tricksters, and other Wily Characters*. New York: Schwartz & Wade, 2008.

Woodson, Carter Godwin. *African Myths and Folk Tales* (Dover Children's Thrift Classics). Mineola, N.Y.: Dover Publications, 2010.

WEB SITES

www.blackpast.org/?q=aah/african-american-museums-united-states-and-canada/
This web site provides links to African American museums around the country.

www.britishmuseum.org/explore/young_explorers/discover/museum_explorer/africa.aspx
Learn more about African life, including gods, goddesses, and death, at this web site of the British Museum.

http://africa.si.edu/
Learn more about African art and culture at this web site of the National Museum of African Art.

www.liverpoolmuseums.org.uk/ism/slavery
Find out about the history of the slave trade that took African culture to the Americas at this UK web site.

PLACES TO VISIT

National Museum of African American History and Culture
National Museum of American History
1400 Constitution Avenue, NW
Washington, DC 20004
http://nmaahc.si.edu
This museum is building its collection for a new building to open
in the near future, focusing on the African American experience.

DuSable Museum of African American History
740 East 56th Place
Chicago, IL 60637
www.dusablemuseum.org
The museum showcases African American history and cultural
contributions.

National Museum of African Art Smithsonian Institution
950 Independence Avenue, SW
Washington, DC 20560
http://africa.si.edu/
This museum focuses on the visual arts of Africa.

FURTHER RESEARCH

If you liked the stories in this book, you could pick one out
and act it. Did you like any of the characters in the book? If so,
you could create a drawing, collage, mask, or sculpture of the
character. Remember that you can use all sorts of materials: shells,
straw, beads, card, wood, and bamboo.

INDEX